Life Before The Pen

The Poems and Songs of A.A. Reid

Lime Tea Books

First published in 2010
By Lime Tea Books
41 The Steils, Edinburgh EH10 5XD

Printed in Scotland by Stewarts of Edinburgh Ltd., Livingston

Design & typsetting: www.contextdesigns.co.uk

ISBN 978-0-9567734-0-1

Foreword

A.A. Reid was born in Ayr, Scotland in 1955, and was educated at Ayr Academy and the University of Edinburgh, where he read politics and modern history. After completing postgraduate studies, he trained as a journalist and magazine editor in Glasgow.

Reid moved with his wife, the award winning writer Antonia Swinson, to London in the early 1980s, where he became a senior public affairs consultant in the City viewing at first hand, some of the most remarkable people and deals of the decade. In the mid 1990s, Reid returned to Scotland, where he made his first forays into expressing himself as an artist singing his original compositions at Haddington Folk Club. Most recently, he formed the rock band Lincoln City, and the folk duo Crumbling Jack, with singer Ian Robertson, exclusively to perform his work.

Today, Reid maintains his career as a management consultant in communication and is also a highly respected single issue political campaigner, founder of the website *www.2020true.com*. He lives with his wife and two children in Edinburgh.

'*Life Before The Pen*' is his first collection of poetry and song.

This first collection of poetry and song is for Antonia Swinson
with love, admiration and gratitude.

A.A. Reid

Edinburgh, November 2010

Selected Poems

III. This Shared Life

IV. Life's Pew:
Politics, Economics & War

Selected Songs

Selected Poems

Life Before the Pen

I suppose the point about pointless prose is just that:
It's pointless.
Yes anding Dante?
Too clever by half
It's been done by John Dɑnne, so...
You having a laugh?
When exactly did forging a connection
Become form without connection?
Turned 30
Ah!
The coward's salvation
Let's hammer out the grants
Replete with salutation
You tick my box
I'll stay onside
Delivery by outcomes
For the half lived life.
Be gone metaphysical sorcerer
And cart your piss-poor pamphlets with you.
Had you but world enough and time
Had you indeed!
Life comes before the pen
Start living my friend.

I. FAME GAME

Horlicks

Should a man change his name to find success
One day he might jist find himself in a mess
And think to himself
Today's the day I will buy myself
A nice, big caramel coloured coat.
Michael Barrymore had one
Bought to prance with filly
Round paddock at Ascot Races
And Saatchi had one too
Bought to fill salesman's till at Savoy Grill
Dining as we do in high places.
Apparently Saatchi's an acronym
Strategic And Targeted Communications Have Impact!
Or some such bollocks
Well what would you expect of Maurice?
A man who would buy himself a coat
The colour of Horlicks

Jeremy Paxman

Twice I've seen Paxo in the flesh
And both times he was putting reason to the test.
First occasion?
The late summer of '92
The wife and I were having a brew and a curry
Getting all in a stew about names for one due
Born on 9/11, seeing it's you.
Seven words or thereabouts
Was all he had to say for himself that night
It must have been twa long hours for one brave lady
Staring back at him, as she was, from our adjoining table.
Fast forward.
It's the late two thousands and pre the crunch
A million quid of tax payers' bread tae munch for Jeremy
Well refreshed and full of gregarious ham
Personality Paxo laid it on wi' jam
tae festival types
About how much he had come
to admire The Royal Family.
A rise for Jeremy
All rise for Sir Jeremy.

McEwan's Special

When I told 'Big Ian' to his face
That his little book lacked grace
He looked quite shocked
But went on to admit
He had taken out the bit
Where rotter interfered with daughter.
Both characters and author
swept away that day as they were
By strong current running
from other side of life's painted veil
And on to Chesilled beach.

Edinburgh Dwellers

Apparently Ian Rankin and Alistair Darling
like to relax of an evening,
drinking Chardonnay
and listening to Coldplay
I bet Chris Martin must be pleased
'Cooler' than ever.
Apparently Sandy McCall Smith
got the idea for 44 Scotland Street
lock, stock and barrel
reading a tale from another city.
And apparently Kate Atkinson is so successful
writing her popularised books
She has not just one personal stalker
she has two.
Which is why, perhaps, apparently
When I walk down Spylaw Road
And J K Rowling sees me coming
She crosses tae the other side of the street
Even when it's no' sunny.

Martin Benson

Just when I thought there could be no more surprises,
I kissed you last summer,
And a bolt shot through my body to the groin.
I guessed you felt it too
How could you not?
Fused together as we were
By a powerful, invisible force
An unknown, unknown
One with the spirits.
Now before a last winter breakfast
of porridge, tea and tonic water
You ask after me
Even while preparing
for one final close-up
Your rendezvous with Death
But not just yet
There's still processing to be done!
Cut.

Brief Encounter

I never actually met Princess Di on the school run to Wetherby
But perhaps she saw me?
She'd obviously had good lunch at The Belfry
And as her car drew near
She plugged me into the national grid I fear
With just one smile.
Tapping driver on the shoulder to slow down as she did
He almost stalled the car
Had it been a plane that he'd been flying
It would have crashed back down to earth
As that angel did
But not then
Not that precious time
Later.

Clown Princess

As we left the Big Top Circus in Monte Carlo town
Stephanie of Monaco tripped over rutted ground
in four inch heels.
Her slim legs were so shapely
her mini skirt was tight
Had she fallen on her arse my friends
it would have made my night
and what a night it was.
Fur coats worn with silk French knickers
Football scarves on royal arse lickers
Reigning prince, grand kids in tow
Grimaldi clowns
made quite the show.

Room at the Top

Christopher Sinclair Stevenson was famous for his dos
And Savile Club at author launch was where I met, guess who?
My favourite book and favourite film and all rolled into one
John couldn't get enough of me, two holes in one then some.
It felt as if we talked all night but minutes it was only
Young man on top, old man below, sharp eyes now tired and lonely
Connected up we got on great: Oh fates thou spread fine table!
But then like Wooster's 'Biffy' Biffen, dear God I lost my Mabel.
"There's someone here that you must meet, come quickly don't delay"
Braine wandered off into the night, again I had no say
I never heard from John again and he heard nought from me
But fate had still one hand to play, before me now I see:

Room At The Top
First Edition
Signed John

Held precious to this day.

Can't Be, Can It

Hoi you!
Hoi you, Big Yin!
Are you the guy off the telly?
The one on 'The Better Sex'?
The wife thinks you look just like Paul McCartney
You look fuck all like Paul McCartney tae me.

Time passes...

She walked in to French cafe
Iconic, known to all
Then stopped and stared mouth open
It's you
My God, it's Paul.
Twas only precious seconds
A lifetime it was not,
But Yoko made that Paris trip
And so her name I drop.

In Jermyn Street where shirts are sold
to those who have much money
I'd often see a well kent face
And this one was a honey.
Stephen Fry, none could deny
Though out without his Laurie
Back from Bruges and well intent
No doubt in saying sorry.

In deep disguise, beard, coat and hat
He stared at me intently
Eyes panicked once he realised
My eyes mocked back most gently.
'Chuffie' wore to good effect
Garb priceless on the telly,
But life had taken frightful turn
So laugh stayed in my belly.

Kensington Songbirds

Warm and sunny outside Barkers
Was the only place to be
As Sade strolled in full, white gown
Regal, black and free
As Lulu pulled her change tae her
I couldna say a word
At M and S in Kensington
Stood one wee Scottish burd
Flown south
and looking
very far from home

Celebrity Stares

It's funny that dread
When life's lived in the head
We tramp the streets in poverty.
No Eye Contact Please

The Good Father

On the occasion of her 18th birthday
She said to her father
'Bring Me The Head Of Dylan Moran'
Not cos you want to
Just cos you can

London Standards 1985

Margaret Duchess of Argyle
And Douglas Fairbanks Junior
Caught the eye, styled to deny
Their era gone forever

Mean Spirit

Please sign this *To Rory*
One day I did plea
This son is a writer, my friend
Just like thee
It hung in the air
And was quite' Pinteresque'
Then the old boy wrote
Two words on his desk
Harold Pinter.

Susan Boyle

Say what you like about Wee Susan Boyle
There's cash in the bank
And she won't need tae toil.

Anyway

Julie Christie Mick Jagger John Major
Grace Jones
Jimmy Savile Jeffrey Archer Alex Salmond
and Griff Rhys Jones
Just some of the well kent faces
From high blown places
I've come across over the years
Who put in a poem
Or a song for that matter
Would have been pointless
As I had nothing to say about them
Well, nothing that was worth saying about them
Anyway

II. THIS SCOTTISH LIFE

Ayr Amusements 1968

BANG! BANG! BANG!
"Right You, OUT!"
'It wisnae me
'HONEST
'It was HIM!'
"I said Out
"NOW!'
'Bastard'
"What did you say?"
'Nothing
'Cunt'
"Come Back YA WEE BASTARD"
'RUN'!!!!

The Wanderer's Return 1998

"May I have a fish on its own"
'A what?'
"And a round pie with fries"
'You mean a single fish and a mince pie supper?'
"Er, that would be the one
"Thank you
"Thank you so much
"Just the thing
"Thanks"
'English Wanker'

Gone Native

Well I say!
Good Lord!
Fucking Mental That Is
Pure Fucking Mental

Life Before Lattes

Monday night was always mince
Tuesday night was stew
Wednesday night was gammon and chips
Thursday night, who knew?
Friday night was cod in crumb
Saturday tea, and a steak took its turn
Sunday roast came with peas and roast tatties
Those were the days
That life before lattes

Just say no

"Haven't we met somewhere before?"
'No'

Oor Library

Andy's the name, past master of spin
Slipped Ayr some dosh, so to leave with a grin
Face on the building, and there for all time
A real heartless bastard, no longer a crime
Shame on Carnegie, and shame on his like
Money can't cleanse, nor draw stench from their shite.

Love at First Sight

Edinbrugh's the brawest toon
It's where I met yir mither
I met her in a stairwell
How her presence made me shiver
Her long, red hair cascaded doon
Like Rita Hayworth in first bloom
Her big blue eyes held out such promise
I knew the bells would ring out for us

Glasgow Central

"Is that yir wife or yir burd?"
'Jist a burd'

Edinburgh Weather

It rained in May, it rained in June
It pished straight doon, one long monsoon
July was hot, and August hotter
Ok I lie, I'm such a rotter
Now here we sit in mid October
Fighting hard to look quite sober
It's turned out fine, we've had a blether
But now outside, lurks Edinburgh weather

Performing Rights

Help I'm being heckled by a little speckled hen
At least I'm no' her husband, being driven round the bend
Lord I've now been heckled, by the man that gives her succour
At least I'm no' goin' hame the night, wi' eyes shut tight tae fuck her

Lecturer Letcherer

Getting back your essay could be quite a tricky thing
The horny little lecturer might fancy a wee fling
A pint or two to warm you up
With eyes that ached for wanton scrub
Pass or fail, well there's the rub
A king fit for king's clothes

Arab Strapped (Scots girl keeps it real)

"Your eyes are like the desert midnight sky
"Your lips are like the dying embers of a blazing, golden sun that has..."
'Och dinna Faris!'

Gag

Help the Aged
And Age Concern Scotland
Have just merged to form
Age Scotland.
Why not Rage Scotland?
"After All I've Done For You!"

Lucky for Some

On 10.10.10
I watched October Sky
And realised why
In school we try
To learn science and maths
Go See!
I wish it was me
Both then, and now
And how

Lifted

Fucking shit and buggeration
Round the roundabout, stagnation
A police car looms
A finger beckons
'Good Evening Sir'
And same to you ya feckin...

Song for Sheldon (When Sad)

Picasso painted pictures
And Van Gogh painted too
Pictures that were put in frames
To share their point of view
Those paintings hang on gallery walls
So silent, yet to us they call
Picasso painted pictures
And Van Gogh painted too

Now Rodin sculpted girls in bronze
Ballerinas with tut tus on
Hair scraped back and pointed toe
Pirouettes then off she goes
This world is full of beautiful sights
That painters paint with all their might
Picasso painted pictures
And Van Gogh painted too

Ken Immortal (Tune: John Peel)

Dae yi Ken McKinlay's secret still
Where all good men may drink their fill
And toast the lassies wi' a gill
'til their breeks stert to leak in the morning.

Fair and Squarely (Alexander Reid 1960)

The gas man cam' tae oor front door
Tae read the meter fairly
Ma mither she was still in bed
Yi see it was sae early
He read the meter then planked doon
A wee rebate o' half a croon
And tae the picters in the toon
Went me and brither Chairley

Fond Farewell

I'll miss you Deb, I'll miss you Debbie
I'll miss that laugh which rang out so ready
I'll miss those eyes, the dance and the sparkle
Now silent the soul, the chat and the prattle

III. THIS SHARED LIFE

Whatever Love Is

When love looms, deep, unspoken,
its thought rules all of life.
Love looms and fear's the token,
the agony sits twice.
Full soul in search of sustenance
doth swell at dead of night.
Resistance,
Where's that option?
The Gods sit on each side.

When love's finger points at wooden heart
and skelfs, why who can say?
Love's hand has formed a trigger,
and fatal blast it may.
What then?
Retreat to virtue?
Descend to madness?
Lust!
When love's door opens just ajar,
its slam, all fingers crush.
What stays inside for keeping
makes hard to exorcise
Fired thoughts.
Desires.
The keening.
Why me? A sacrifice.
As pain turns into torture,
and sad reports it must.
All thoughts of lust may wither,
but this time,
love's been,
sussed.

Toxic Blonde

'She's not all bad', well fair enough
Let's concentrate on all good stuff
And figure out just what she says and does
And how she says and does it
To get away with all the other guff.
Too often we admire the blonde without
And fail to get a handle
On the chippie little brunette within.
She dyed and rose again?
God help us all
God help us all.

Penny Stocks

Isn't it funny how some couples, coalesce quite happily together,
in a peculiar form of hell?
And isn't it funny how some mothers trade their daughters' stock,
intent or hoping that it will become a worthless sell?
And isn't it funny that it isn't very funny, not at all.
Sell. Sell. Sell.

Family Betrayal

It's not so much the act of betrayal, as the way that it's done
Delivered as 'fun', by a prodigal son.
It's not so much the money that's tasted
As the way that you're placed at, a gateway to hell.
Casual betrayal's not casual at all
Its roots take when small, when you were having a ball.
With family, betrayal's a dangerous game
Life's never the same, whatever the gain.
Oh for sure you may think that you've won
But time takes its turn, and the bank's had a run.

Harrods Bomb

How I wish I could turn back time.
How I yearn to have read those signs
And stopped fates' train in its track.
Sad to say there can be no amends
Try as I might I cannot ring-fence
That car from my sight
Suspiciously parked as it was by a rusher
Fit only my friends, for last ride to the crusher.
In Knightsbridge?
Bugger!

New Best Friend

I don't know if I should mention this...
But he's a very good listener, is old Rembrandt.
True, there's always that rather supercilious stare to contend with..
And that slightly mocking look in his eyes
But time after time he draws me back
For a brief and confidential chat
My confessor
Whose parting shot to me is always reassuringly the same.
Tosser.

Knobs

Sometimes a man reaches for the top, and pulls it off
Only to discover he has 'man-boobs', and a terminal smoker's cough.
How the Gods call time, on ambitious, single minds, with knobs on.

Greek Sentiment

Broken feral cat cries bleating from the gutter
Just a curiosity to Peroulades mothers
We die alone.
Get over it.

Suicide Watch

Time doth steal, and time doth wither
A serpent's tongue, from life we slither
Try Harder.
For time will heal, and time will favour
Just hang on, there's life to savour
Try Harder.
Must Try Harder.

Saint or Sinner

A patron saint, a patron sinner
A close run race, a likely winner.
A reputation, come the grave
Too late, my friend.
Too late, to save.

Reclining Nude

Respectable people, cruise the beach and stare
'Look over there... oh my God he's bare!'
A welcome dip, he rises from the water, and walks towards them
The ambush sprung

Unexpected Pleasure

Beware young man, beware
For there she dances
Not as pretty as she once was
Not as firm as she once was
Nor as sane as she once was
And, long before breakfast
Draws a candle from the fridge

Sensible Shoes

Worn by top photographer
While shagging unshorn sheep
Were snugly fitted desert boots
On naked spindly feet.
Ewe.

Mayhem in Morningside
(RICHARD ALERT)

November snow brings a mortal blow
Dear God On Earth they've closed Waitrose!

Control

If left alone at Christmas against your wishes
Try turning the control dial to nought
And serving other dishes

Season's Greetings

At Christmas, spare a thought
For the man who has tintinus for Christmas
Not just tinsel.
And at Christmas, spare a thought
For the woman that gets a black eye for Christmas
Not just a mince pie.
And at Christmas, spare a thought for the Christmas
That is just another Christmas
Since a loved one dropped
A life went pop
And the whole world stopped.

Lost Youth

What is saw is what is seen
A page that forms a magazine
Of lust and want and need for party,
Or is it charity?
Too late, my friend
Much too late.

The Margin of Error
(Required reading for policy makers)

When ninety nine in a hundred
cannot read,
Whitehall has this strange conceit.
'That number fills us not with terror,
'Come on old boy
'It's the margin of error'.
Now David Cameron knows what's what
And frankly doesn't give a jot.
The Tory child can buy and pay for
A detailed look to find a saviour
Those other kids can just get lost
Good Lord, old boy
Have you seen the cost?

www.2020true.com

IV. LIFE'S PEW
Politics, Economics & War

Political Channels

I once asked Walter Campbell
if he would ever visit British soldiers
grievously wounded in battle
Ming, for it was he,
looked at me quite crossly,
 and most put out said:
"No.
"Certainly Not"
And so Ming had to go, and go he did.
End of Dynasty, change channels.
I once pointed out to Gordon Brown,
A key component of Blair's legacy
was there should be no Brown legacy
Other than as his Chancellor.
Communication plan was written
Fifteen points and delivered
to fingers famously well bitten.
Passing all sentry and sweet for early entry
It was followed to the letter.
And didn't we all feel better, for a time?
But the bully's rule, made empty fools of all of us.
My apology
My apologies
Let's welcome back democracy.

Black Monday

On Black Monday I was in the City
Expecting to ha'e lunch
Get all the nitty gritty
But it was a windy day
and the paper didnae show
Trust the fucking Guardian
That was a blow.
As the lift cranked doon tae deserted streets below
I heard this man intone
"No one could have forseen this coming".
It wisnae Fred Goodwin
And it wisnae Crosby either
He's a clever little beggar
And looks just like a Caesar
But it might as well have been
For all that I had seen wi' James and all.
Lehman and the lemmings have been
A long time coming,
Trust me dear friends
On that day it was already up and running.
When a man marches tae the beat of his own drum
Other men fall silent
If there's money tae be won.

Clever Clogs (Pushing Product)

The expression: 'Thatcher's Children'
I coined for a purpose
Scot Am, MORI, and the whole fucking circus.

Scottish Bankers

Many years before Hornby
let little Duggie stray,
The speccy little manager
took time out to say,
Colleague Crosby has no prayer
Top Man Appointment
No Catholic Need Apply.
Rangers or Celtic
Hearts or Hibs
Ask me no questions
I'll tell you no fibs.

Ketchup

I once marched through the streets of Edinburgh
Carrying a banner I'd made at home that very September
It read:
>*TONY BLAIR*
>*HE'S NOT THE MESSIAH*
>*HE'S A VERY NAUGHTY BOY!*

Ask the wife
She'd tell you.

I once had the big idea
Every anti-war protestor
Shouldn't jist let things fester
A ketchup satchet in yir pocket
And like a rocket
Should you ever bump into Tony B
It would be
"Tony Old Boy
"You've got blood on your hands Mr Blair."
That was to be the punch-line greeting
Upon that meeting
Followed by a hankie on loan.

Then one day in Margiotta
And quite the fluke for
'Tony Blair's having lunch
'Just up the road in San Luca'.
Sure enough his erse had been seated
And he had been greeted
From my favourite seat
Quite the treat
But us destined not to meet.

In time I rode through the streets o' Edinburgh
In Ainsworth's military convoy
Oh boy! It was just before Megrahi
And Admiral Fitzgerald, a yankee,
Didn't look too happy
He didn't look too happy, not at all.
From Governor's Mansion near airport
Tae Edinburgh Castle
There was never any hassle
For we never stopped once.
I was having so much fun
On sniper's bullet run
I took a funny turn.
Twice.

What price Ketchup then, my friend?
What price Ketchup then?
And what price?
The lost eye
The lost leg
The lost everything.

Holy Smoke!

"They're speaking in tongues in New Malden".
(*Alpha contagion grips Chiswick*)
"God is always such good company at a dinner party".
(*Mrs Rowan Williams keeps it unreal*)
"I'm a pretty straight sort of guy".
(*War criminal turns Catholic*)

Alastair Campbell

Apparently Alastair Campbell at the age of 53
Disnae need tae get up in the night to go and hae a pee
He claims he's more like a man of 40, or even 39
I think the bugger's full o' shit, and should be doing time

Female of the Species

If I had a million pounds
I would happily hand it over
For Cherie Blair
If she was for sale that day.
Such fine art
And I would gaze at her wondrously
Last thing at night
And first thing in the morning
Come what may
Euan Uglow was a genius
And what can I say?
Too bad the burd in his picture
Led a silly little runt astray.
Poor Dorian
Poor Dorian Gray.

Disnaeland

Disnae vote Tory?
Tick
Disnae pay any tax?
Tick
Disnae matter a fuck tae anyone?
Tick
Welcome to Disnaeland
And thank you
For voting
Scottish Labour.
Tick

Breaking News

I hate to be the one to tell you this
But up close and personal
Margaret Thatcher
Was really rather beautiful
And had lovely, shapely ankles

Comedy Turn

Close your eyes and really listen
Then tell me what you hear
Tony Blair sounds just like Julian Clary
Oh dearie, dearie me.

Tory Conference

"Where *exactly* do you live?"
'I rather think you are trying to place me'

Tory Marriage (Constituency Matters)

Isn't this just wonderful
Isn't this just great
A 30 mile tail back for a bit of wedding cake.
Brage Brage

Isn't this too splendid
But isn't it quite mad
A damsel pushing forty
And a fat Sir Galahad?
Brage Brage

Aha... isn't this too heavenly
Oh isn't this quite neat
The cash to turbo charge career
And purchase family seat!
Brage Brage

Oh isn't this too fabulous
Oh isn't this too swell
A sonnet then a disco
Oh shit and fucking hell.
Brage Brage

Political Luck

Political luck is where it all matters
Without it my friend, career sits in the tatters.
Ashdown, Kennedy, Campbell and Clegg
Only the one got to hatch from the egg.
Portillo, Davis, Cameron and Hague
Only the one's 'Path To Number Ten' laid.
 Milliband, Milburn, Johnson and Reid
Not up to the task, nor the dirtiest deed.

Women's Lib

When Nick Clegg was asked,
How many women he'd have
In the first Con-Dem Cabinet,
He may very well have replied:
Of course I have no certainty...
But my very best guess would be...
A whole lot less...than thirty.
Floreat Etona, old boy
Let Eton Flourish.

Cacti Calling (Youth Re-Lit)

One that should have made
Nick Clegg's Desert Island Discs
Is 'Firestarter' by The Prodigy.
Forget the nicotine patches
It's not so much the fags
Nick couldn't live without
It's the matches!

Political Dancing
(Tune: A Laws Unto Himself)

Explaining himself to his constituency
The talk and tone, was one of poverty
No money, for it had long since gone
Mortgaged, just like all those forlorn.
The bought and paid-for gaff in France
A missing spin, from that political dance.
An early return is now what is promised
No room on the card for a Doubting Thomas
The call must go out for 'The Mildest Rebuke'
As we can't take the floor for 'The Political Crook'.

The Soldier's Farewell

Mary, Mary, Mary.
I love thee most contrary
I'm 'never here' most every day
 Never there with you to play
On the Road to Mandalay
Mary, Mary, Mary.

Mary, Mary, Mary.
I love thee so contrary
I'm always on the old night shift
Never there tae gi' a lift
Or even have a lover's tiff
Mary, Mary, Mary.

Mary, Mary, Mary.
I love thee most contrary
I put my life in danger here
Summon up the battle rear
Never show an ounce of fear
Mary, Mary, Mary.

Mary, Mary, Mary
I loved thee so contrary
The shrapnel took out stomach wall,
Too my face, then took my balls
Mary, Mary, Mary.

Political Fun (Clever Clogs 2)

Does the march in youth to Sergeant Pepper
Make you, old boy, the political leper?
And lo, the dirty deed was done
The stage now set for political fun.
What say you Sir, to an Arctic Monkey
The life on hold needs no political flunkey.

Land Economy

Three bedrooms in a block of four
Two gairdens front and rear
The council hoose in Harold's Land
Was built to Tory cheers
"They've Never Had It So Good!'
But that was then
And this is now
Where housing knits the Tory brow.
That land is rich
That land is treasure
We'll have to bring in other measures.
Thinks.
Let's clear the buggers out of there
They've too much time to stop and stare
Our Big Society won't stand it
And new found Tory votes demand it.
They'll give it up
And give it now
No Keys For Life
Our sacred vow.

Spin Cycle

Nasty Nick
Calamity Clegg
I Agree With Nick
Political Death

War's Over 1950

(In memory of J.D.M Reid, shot down 1943, age 19)

Are you coming tae bed?
Aye. I'll be up in a minute
But leave the door open
Jim's no' back yet.

Bard's Brief

Had we but world enough and time?
We have indeed
Life comes before the pen
Start living my friend!

Selected Songs

I. SONGS FROM LINCOLN CITY (PART ONE)

Longing

Two days out from Lincoln City, a fire to keep me warm
No arms to hold me through the night, until Nebraska morn'
Guess I'm longing
A marriage bed creaks like the wind, to gather up a storm
And passion stirs a perfect wave, to break, one body formed
Fevered longing

I'm longing after you
I'm longing after you
I'm longing after you
Fevered longing, longing

I long to know just how I feel about the love that's done
I long to know just how I feel about the love to come
Longing
I long to know what happens, will I put my mind to rest?
I long to know the final score, how will I do...my best?
Longing, longing

I long to touch your body, then pull it close to mine
I long to taste your milky skin, then drink from it fine wine
I long to lay my arm across, the contour of your breast
I long to hear the bird awake, then sing out from the nest

I'm longing after you

That Other Guy

I've loved you since I first set eyes on you
I've loved you every second, that's the truth
I love the way the sun falls on your face
I love the way it's God that gives you grace
And I love the way your smile lights up a room
And I love the way you make us sing in tune
My dearest friend may hold you in his arms
My dearest friend won't do you any harm

Just because I love you, doesn't mean we're not all friends
And just because I need you, doesn't mean a heart won't mend
And just because your picture hangs, on someone else's wall
Doesn't mean you can't be mine that other guy may fall

I love the way a trail runs from your scent
I love the way that every word is meant
I love the way you question right from wrong
I love the way you move your life along
And I love the way you turn the water tap
And I love the way you drive a horse and trap
I love every single freckle on your skin
And I love the way you pour that glass for him

Just because I love you, doesn't mean we're not all friends
And just because I need you, doesn't mean a heart won't mend
And just because your picture hangs, on someone else's wall
Doesn't mean a God-dam thing , that other guy may fall

Heaven knows it makes a grown man cry
Heaven knows to have your life run dry
Telling lies, I tell a friend that she's the one for you
Telling lies won't ever make that true
Lord I know you'd teach our children well
Lord I know you'd teach our children well
Lord I know our table would be swell
Lord I know our table would be swell

It's the way the moments hang when we are on our own
It's the way the hours fly by when love has found a home
It's the way my spirits soar and laughter fills the air
It's the way we walk outside and people stop and stare

I bless the day you took your marriage vows
I bless the day you took your marriage vows
I blessed that day but God look at me now
I blessed that day but God look at me now

Just because the years go by I can't give up on hope
Just because the years go by I won't hang from a rope
And just because he turned the hands and got you before me
Doesn't mean that other guy won't fall and you'll be free

I guess I'll always love you for all time
I guess I'll always love you for all time
I guess I have to pray one day you're mine
I guess I have to pray one day you're mine

When we go out hunting there's a firearm in my hand
And when we go out fishing there's a lake that's deep and calm
But when we get to talking there's a point that I must leave
Lord I'm only human, and my heart sits on my sleeve

I guess I'll always love you for all time
I guess I'll always love you for all time
I guess I have to pray one day you're mine
I guess I have to pray one day you're mine

Hanging by a thread had found me reaching for the scissors
In hanging by that thread, I found a lie, distorted mirrors
In hanging by that thread I found a shotgun in my hand
My brother's life for happiness, the hand I had to call

And just because I love you, doesn't mean we're not all friends
Just because I need you, doesn't mean a heart won't mend
And just because your picture hangs on my twin brother's wall
Doesn't mean you can't be mine, that other guy might fall

I've loved you since I first set eyes on you
I've loved you since I first set eyes on you
I've loved you, every second, that 's the truth
I've loved you, every, second, that's the truth

Don't Turn Your Back
On Me This Way

When I look in your eyes, I feel so uneasy
For what is hurting there, deep down inside
Tender love has flown, and we both know the reason
No more that season, gone, no return
But love has a passion that burns back around
Love has a meaning, to grasp and pin down

Don't walk away and leave me here, with only heartache
Come back and let me know you'll stay
Please stop and think about, the love I still believe in
Don't turn your back on me this way

I should have promised less, can't you forgive me?
It really doesn't matter now, what's done is done
We can set it right, of this I know it
Stay, we can grow it, a second chance

For love has a passion that burns back around
Love has a meaning to grasp and pin down
Don't walk away and leave me here with only heartache
Come back and let me know you'll stay
Please stop and think about, the love I still believe in
Don't turn your back on me this way.

Going Back to Arizona

Sometimes in life, you must wake and look around you
Sometimes in life, you must see what you must see
The game's not worth the candle
It's time to turn the key

And so I know I'm going back to Arizona
I know that's where my spirit wanders free
The desert sand that shimmers, like the finest silver sea
I know I'll find that peace of mind, been missing all these years

Sometimes in life, there's a voice that speaks within you
Sometimes in life, there's a voice you can't ignore
It's time to make that journey
It's time to get on home

It's never easy to break the ties that bind you
The path can be crazy hard to find
But nothing can keep me from reaching my journey's end
Only the sands of time

And so I know I'm going back to Arizona
I know that's where my spirit wanders free
The desert sand that shimmers like the finest silver sea
I know I'll find that peace of mind, been missing all these years
I know I'll find that peace of mind, been missing all these years.

Safe in Your Arms

You are always by my side
There is no where I can hide
In my mind I feel a strength, I never knew before
I can climb a mountain top
See the world, and never drop
To the darkness, down below
Your love will keep me in its glow

Safe in your arms, you are the heart of me,
The part of me, that sets my spirit free
You keep me warm and secure,
Forever in my life, a shining light,
That's showing me the way

Time was a drag for me, the mirror was no friend
Life was a loser's game, but now my heart can mend

I was lost and now I find
One true love that isn't blind
To the key that says I can, lose weakness, make new plans
Now I know that I can bring, to the world a song to sing
And share forever, in my life
A love that holds me through the night

Safe in your arms, you are the heart of me
The part of me that sets my spirit free
You keep me warm and secure
Forever in my life, a shining light
That's showing me the way.

Make It Last Awhile

Being young sits doggone well
And hell I know your life is swell
And each day spawns a man who's hearty
Life for you just one big party
Liquor, beer and margarita
Find a girl who'd love to meet you
Figure out how to pop the question
About the stuff her Pa won't mention

Women love a long slow burn
And young man learn to take your turn
Put more kindling on the fire
To ensure your heart's desire
Bourbon, gin and neat scotch whisky
Kindly stuff that makes girls frisky
See her through her mother's eyes
A gent should make it last awhile

Make it last awhile, make it last awhile
Go that extra mile, make it last awhile
Make it last awhile, make it last awhile
Show that southern style, make it last awhile

Listen up and hear my talking
Soon through life you'll do your walking
Brandy, rum and sarsaparilla
Cuddle up to your own pillow
Lose the booze that makes you holler
Demon fights won't give you bother
Show her you've got southern style
The kind who'll make it last awhile

Independence Day

Instrumental

Commissioned by A.A. Reid

Nothing Would Have Been Any Old Fun At All

Without your love I don't know where I'd be
Without your love I don't know where I'd be
Drifting on the sea of life I'd be
Drifting on the sea of life I'd be

For nothing would have been any old fun at all
No nothing would have been any old fun at all
Without your love to make me walk so tall
Nothing would have been any old fun at all

How you found me I will never know
How you found me I will never know
Bringing here the joy to make me glow
Bringing here the joy to make me glow

Life can be a rollercoaster ride
Life can be a rollercoaster ride
Until I die I want you by my side
Until I die I want you by my side

Made to Measure

My dear ma she said to me
Son I'm done looking after thee
It's time you left this house of mine
To look for a wife that's sweet as wine

For love can never be made to measure
Any old fool won't find this treasure
Love needs a hunting and tracking down
No good woman's just hanging around

So I caught the train and headed for the city
Found me a girl who was warm and witty
Took her home as my wedded wife
Now she's known as the trouble and strife

Built us a home and started a family
Three boys first then a girl to look after me
All sitting up in a pick-up truck
Lord I've been blessed by that lady called luck

Now my boy's hitting four and twenty
Eyeing the girls who are mighty flirty
Looking out for the precious one
Who's going to be his bride and give him a son

Catherina

Catherina tell me have you seen her
The beauty of Athena
The girl who changed my life
We got taking
Then we went a walking
Oh it was really shocking
How hard in love I fell

Catherina tell me have you seen her
The beauty of Athena
The girl who changed my life
We were joking
Soon our love was smoking
Then my heart got broken
The girl had changed my life

But she had to go back
On the railroad track
To the hills of Cincinnati
So I'm waiting alone,
By the telephone
For a long distance call
From my one and only Rena

I've Been Happier Almost Any Time Than Now

Love plays a waiting game to keep you in its thrall
You spend your life looking out for her, waiting for that call
But when love comes it often leaves you when you're least aware
You look around, there's no one there, there's nothing left to share
When a lover goes, it's never easy
In the afterglow of a mad affair I can safely say
I've been happier almost any time than now

Now love's gone I haven't got the heart for it
With love gone I want no more a part of it
I've been there so many times and fouled it up
It's true, I know, I'll never love again
When a lover goes
It's never easy
In the afterglow of a sad affair
I can safely say
I've been happier almost any time than now

Burn Out Blues

Woke up again this morning, I couldn't get out of bed
Woke up again this morning and it's doing in my head
I've got the burn out blues again
Oh yes the burn out blues again

Tried to get a motor turning
Tried to make a songbird sing
Tried to move on up and pick the fruit that life can bring
But I've got the burn out blues again
Oh yes the burn out blues again

Standing in the shower with soap suds round my feet
I'm standing in the shower, oh God another day to greet
With those burn out blues again
Oh yes the burn out blues again

Chased the burn 'til sunset, then danced in clubs till dawn
My dancing days are done now, each stay starts with a yawn
And those burn out blues again
Oh yes the burn out blues again

Woke up again this morning, a little gas there in my tank
Woke up again this morning, squeezed some juice then rang the bank
But I got the burn out blues again
Oh yes the burn out blues again.

Leaving

The good Lord they will tell you, gives us three score years and ten
Time travels fast enough, I hear, before the last amen
I guess we reconcile, repent the loss that we must bear
Except those thoughts of leaving you, all made without a care
I left the path I needed, chose the 'I want' path instead
Conceit said "I can always" but the sacrifice has bled
The mystery still taunts me, as it's taunted those before
I could have saved our life for sure walked through an open door

The Gods on Mount Olympus clearly knew a trick or two
The Oracle could call upon a vision, always true
Our fate is not to know just what they have for us in store
Our hell is not to know just what the point of us is for
Our missing life still haunts me as it has haunted those before
Our missing life still finds me screaming quietly by the door
And missing peace of mind still plays on loop between my mind
The path we might have trod forked to a road without a sign

Do you ever stop and think about the total sum we've lost?
Do you ever stop and add the final commas to the cost?
Do you ever pause or question, does that light bulb switch turn on
Do you ever see that failure goes back to the day you are born?
Do you ever stop and think about the mysteries of life?
Do you ever source perfection as the root of human strive?
Do you ever clock that lying to yourself won't set you free?
Do you ever think the problem all along might just be me?
The good Lord they will tell you, gives us three score years and ten
Time travels fast enough, I fear, before the last amen
I guess we reconcile, repent the loss that we must bear
Except those thoughts of leaving you all made without a care.

Vanitas Vanitatum

Instrumental

Commissioned by A.A. Reid

That's What Life's About

Should a tear fall on your pillow, I will dry your eyes
A cloud burst on a summer's day, I will clear the skies
When you're sick, I'll hold your hand
When you're poor, I'll pay demands
I will always understand, cos that's what life's about

When this world has made you weary, I will ice some tea
Take you to the movies, If there's one to see
When your smile has lost all trace I'll put it back upon your face
With perfume and some pretty lace, cos that's what life's about

Flatter when you're feeling low
Chatter if the company's slow
Leave you with a healthy glow, cos that's what life's about
Swear to never be a bore, someone you will aye adore
Revere you when you're 94, cos that's what life's about

Should a tear fall on your pillow, I will dry your eyes
A cloud burst on a summer's day, I will clear the skies
When you're sick I'll hold your hand
When you're poor I'll pay demands
I will always understand
Cos that's what life's about.

II. SONGS FROM LINCOLN CITY (PART TWO)

I Can Hardly Bear To Think Of You

I can hardly bear to think of you, it really throws my mind
For a feeling rises up in me, from a place that's so sublime
And the wonder is I never knew that such a state exists
A fevered kiss that e'er insists, without so much a kiss

I can see you with a waking eye, just someone I adore
And I know I'd walk a million miles, to lay my love before
Someone I could always love and cherish evermore
With body, mind and riven soul, what all in life is for

I can only pray the Lord above, you feel the way I do
That I might see it in the way you move, or hold my eyes so true
A feeling that not you nor I could ever dare deny
A feeling that can take on wing and soar a mountain high

I can hardly bear to think of you, another moment more
I can hardly bear to dream of you, the fox might hear my roar
A waking call in endless small of night that's dark and blue
A beating heart, a waking heart, that thinks of only you

I can hardly bear to think of you, it really throws my mind
For a feeling rises up in me, a feeling , a feeling that 's so sublime
And the wonder is I never knew that such a state exists
A fevered kiss, that e'er insists, without so much a kiss.

I Found A Voice

Who would have thought, just yesterday
That I could feel this way
Who could have thought, the other day
That I could heal this way
Yet here I am, just someone knew
Who's starting out from now
Yes here I am, who always knew
I'd tell the world: 'Watch out!'

I found a voice, a whispered voice
I know I can believe in
I found a voice, a treasured voice
And now the world can see that
I'm not alone, not far from home
I take my spirit with me
I'm starting out, beginning now
To take my own long journey
I found a voice

Who would have thought, that little me
Had so much more to say
Who could have thought that silly me
Could offer up a prayer
To get it right, put up a fight
And not put up with crap
To say: "Heh You! Leave me alone!
"I'm calling time! A wrap!"

I found a voice, a treasured voice
I know I can believe in
I found a voice a precious voice
And now the world can see that
I'm not alone, not far from home
I take my spirit with me
I'm starting now, beginning now
To take my own long journey
I found a voice.

If Heaven Came to Earth

The girl I knew I'd marry, and babes for sure to carry
The Lord above decreed it would be you
And so it came to pass, I married you fair lass
And pledged dear love until my dying day

If heaven came to earth
If death turn back to birth
I wouldn't want to be here without you
If rainfall fell as wine
If it always turned out fine
I wouldn't want to see it without you

Now as the years go on
Good looks one day be gone
Still all I'll see's the beauty that is you
The eyes may well grow dim
We may move without much vim
But all the while I'll dance through life with you

For if heaven came to earth
If death turned back to birth
I wouldn't want to be here without you
And if rainfall fell as wine
If it always turned out fine
I wouldn't want to see it without you

Somethin'

Now lookie here just the other day
I went out, without a prayer, with nuthin'
I sure had nuthin'
So I asked the dear Lord to stay on my side
Make sure my eyes were open and wide for somethin'
And we found somethin'

Chorus
For we found wine, wine, wine,
We found wine, wine, wine
And we had a good time, time, time
Had a good time, time, time
Yes we had a good time, time, time
As we drank wine

So how'd that occur, I hear you ask
How'd the Lord go about that task with nuthin'
He sure had nuthin'
Well first it was water, then it was wine
He wanted to be sure that I had a good time with somethin'
And that sure was somethin'
For we drank wine, wine, wine...

Then I had me a thought, not an ounce of fear
Asked the dear Lord for a crate of beer
That's somethin', that sure'd be somethin'
But he just laughed and said that I jest
Water into wine's what I do best, a thumpin'
And that sure was somethin'
So we drank wine, wine, wine...

Twa Pipers

Oh the wedding bells have pealed, and the couple their first reel
And the guests already half way to half fu'
When twa pipers slip away, to raise a glass Weh Heh
And stand tall proud at famous Royal Oak

Chorus
Royal Oak, Royal Oak, the wee bar that ain't no joke
It's the warmest, dearest snug in all the land
Where the staff keep all things light
And wee May cries "Heh Nae fights!"
It's the warmest, dearest snug in all the land

Well the tourists wander in
And the locals give a grin
They've been sitting tight since 1863
They'll be going hame quite soon
Once they land and peg balloon
But for now they're staying where God meant they be.

Now this fellow got quite drunk
Thought that he'd become a monk
For his wife, and girlfriend said they'd had enough
Repent he would his sins
Scour his balls each day with vim
Well it serves the bugger right for drinking gin

When this fellow slipped to floor and cried
The wife had shown the door
It was really, very, very, very, sad
Well the future's somewhat grim
But with luck she'll stick with him
And he'll be back to sup a pint or four

The Duke

His Ducal land spreads wide and that poor guy has his pride
Five hundred thousand acres ain't all fun
To make it worth his while he must keep the land in style
Pay no taxes not with smart accounting

Chorus
He's not so much your grace as a disgrace
He's keeping all the money owed to you
He's pushed the land offshore, paying tax is such a bore
Not so much your grace as a disgrace

Since 2009 with the country in declne
Our transport, schools and hospitals eat shit
While that wily Duke stays rich, the UK life of debt's a bitch
And he's laughing all the way to Lichtenstein

Now's the time for cutting free, tax the land not you and me
For this joke is wearing mighty thin
And the Duke should now think on, for his House of Lords has gone
And revolt can sweep out history

Bar Room Woman

Well she caught my eye
Bought her a drink then a room for hire
Oh so easy.
I thrust my key into the lock
Showed her everything I got
And when she went to work I cried out baby
Don't break this ache

Well she dripped some wax
Sure enough near a heart attack
Oh so sleazy
She had me tied up like a steer
Saw my eyes were full of fear
But when she cut me loose
I cried out baby
Don't break this ache

This Life

I love this life it's a beautiful day
I love this life most everyway
Musical laughs and lovely smiles
Make me feel happy all of a while
I love this life it's a beautiful day
I love this life most every way

I love this life it's a beautiful day
I love this life most every way
Babes sing like angels and are so nice
I love their ways no need to think twice

I love this life it's a beautiful day
I love this life whatever it may
Bring with each promise, deliver and say
That all cool feelings are here now to stay
I love this life it's a beautiful day
I love this life most every way.

Huckleberry Finn

I saw that look that crossed upon your face
The love we had, had clearly left no trace
You saw me as a hog stuck in my stile
The verdict called, swear God I'd had my trial

For sure I weren't no Huckleberry Finn
And true our life at times was pretty grim
But loving you aint' never been no sin
Sure I weren't no Huckleberry Finn

We can find a boat a paddle too
We can find adventure out the blue
We can catch that spirit ain't too late
Stick the finger to the hands of fate

This great country has a lot of miles
There are places we can hit the tiles
Oh for sure I'll bring out all your smiles
Just come back and say you'll stay awhile

The Poacher

Chorus
Heh let's open a bottle of wine
Heh grab a fiddle and step in time
Heh where's a partner for the dance room floor?
Hips keep a rocking won't keep no score

Heh I've been out on the hunt this day
Had me some luck got a stag in bay
Poaching sure gives me my say
Screw the system where it plays
Heh little goose got a taste for bread
Stretch out your neck and I'll grab your head
Bags in the bushes for the journey home
Pluck you for supper let the table groan

Folks call me Bob but that ain't my name
Living this life gives me no shame
If you've got an issue find a James to blame
Trust me, to-morrow I'll be there the same
Out there roaming on Richmond Hill
Taking all in as the park grows still
Find me a critter with a likely bill
Then home for supper and a welcome gill.

Clover

I've been trying to work out for some time now
What it is you people got to shout 'bout
Seems to me the system turns you over
Life for you no fucking bed of clover
Grey old people eat you up for breakfast
Fit them up then ship them out to Texas
Heh those boomers ain't no more life's nexus
Crash and burn a legacy so feckless
I believe that come the revolution
There must be some answers some solution
All that feudal crap is just pollution
All those Princelings just a drag a nuisance
I've been trying to work out for some time now
What it is you people got to shout 'bout
Seems to me the system turns you over
Life for you no fucking bed of clover

Licentious

I like the way you're walking
I like the things you're talking
I like the way you're moving
I love the way you're grooving
You make me so licentious
You make me so licentious
There ain't no room for friendship
You make me so licentious
I love the way you tipple
Those eyes, that nose and... nipples
In sending out those ripples
You're turning me a cripple
Bring those kisses over here right now
Get on down let's see you take a bow
Take me where the pleasure pictures play
Push me in spotlight hear me bray
You're making me licentious
And there ain't no room for friendship
You're making me licentious.

Sinners

You can see it in our eyes, catch it in our looks
Read the way our furtive tastes are catered for in books
We're all sinners
You can see it in our walk, hear it in our talk
Clock the way we rise each day and set this world to shock
For we're all sinners
Yes we're all sinners
We're all sinners
We're not beginners, no no,
We're siren singers
Want some kisses? Try those ones called French
Found some morals? Heh look down that trench
For we're all sinners
Yes we're all sinners
Got a dirty secret? Ain't we all!
Some may be real tiny, most ain't small
The apple and the floosie, man must fall
So just get in among it, have a ball
For we're all sinners.

Lying

The fool likes to say that he knows everything
'Heh Man. Relax! Take each day what it brings'
It's fine to be 'cool' when you see where you're going
But people like me don't get the same growing

Trapped in a cage and yet chased by a lion
Nobody knows that inside you're dying
See my face, and see that I'm crying
So why do you say that in life I'm just lying

Help me dear Lord, can't you hear what I'm saying
Don't ask me to wait, for I'm way beyond praying
No help for a man, dear God it's a slaying
Answer me this, if your son is for saving

Trapped in a cage and yet chased by a lion
Nobody knows that inside you're dying
See my face and see that I'm crying
So why do you say that in life I'm just lying.

Don't Leave Me

Walking in the park, a chill runs to my heart
You're leaving?
The words you had to say: "You going to be OK?"
You're leaving??
Don't Leave Me
A hand goes to my back, no point in turning back
You're leaving
"Walk over here," you say. For eyes will pry away
Filling up ain't 'cool', don't want to look a fool
For you're leaving.
You're the one who always got the looks
Meeting someone else was all it took
Pull the plug, call time and close the book
For our life together, it don't suit
So you're leaving.
The rain runs through my head
I think of us in bed
And all the things you said
The stories we had read
But, you're leaving.

The Ballad of Abelard and Héloise

Abelard and Héloise they both set out to please
Fall in love in this old world? It's rarely called a breeze
Tripping off the high-wire or tipping off trapeze
Whichever way it happens, love gits you on your knees

Abe and Elle poor souls, if I may be so bold
Were looking out for somethin', that I for one call nothing
Fall in love that hard just puts you off your guard
Best stay down the booser than go through life a loser

Cleopatra did it, and Tony did it too
It's figured out in prisons, beneath the eyes of screws
Whatever way it comes by, sure 'nough it makes you blue
Getting off in this old world is just a day to rue

Tristan and Isolde if I may be so bold
Were set up good for something, that I for one call nothing
Fall in love that hard just puts you off your guard
Best stay down the booser than go through life a loser.

An Independent Nation Once Again

When Scotland lost its sovereignty, that nation old and proud
Protest did echo o'er the land, and oft was spoke aloud
Now time has turned again, my friend, one nation and one heart
And Scottish independence, once more is coming back

For independent nation, is how we see ourselves
An independent nation, with all the world to tell
About this Scotland, this dear old Scotland
An independent nation once again

Time passes and we count and bless our neighbours and our friends
One nation and one people in shared recognised intent
We'll play our part in this great world, no need to make amends
Our sons and daughters freedom, we will fight for and defend

Cry out for Scotland, this dear old Scotland
An independent nation once again
Cry out for Scotland, this dear old Scotland
An independent nation once again

Music credits

Songs From Lincoln City (Part One) was recorded at Banana Row Studios, Eyre Place, Edinburgh, between January and August 2008. Music direction, arrangements and supervision by Christopher Sessions; studio engineer, Nick Moore; mastering engineer, now at Air Studios, London, Matt Colton. Special thanks go to Craig Hunter and his staff of Banana Row.

All the songs on the recording were composed by A.A. Reid, apart from the two instrumentals, *Independence Day* and *Vanitas Vanitatum*, which were commissioned from Christopher Sessions, and the melody line of *That Other Guy* which was predominantly written in the studio by Christopher Sessions, Ali Campbell, Micah Brashear and A.A. Reid. David Crystal co wrote the lyric of Burn Out Blues.

All the vocals were delivered by Ali Campbell, apart from *Made to Measure* and *Nothing Would Have Been Any Old Fun At All*. Guest singers on those numbers were Ella Swinson Reid and Rod Sessions, who also played guitar.

Micah Brashear played double bass on the tracks, with Ali Campbell on pedal steel guitar. Drummer Calum McIntyre played on *That Other Guy, Made to Measure and Make It Last Awhile*. Dan Cotton played drums on *Don't Turn Your Back On Me This Way, Safe in Your Arms* and *Going Back to Arizona*. Tony Higgins played drums on *Nothing Would Have Been Any Old Fun At All*.

All the other instruments on the tracks, including keyboard, guitar, mandolin, violin and accordion were played by Christopher Sessions, who also played bass guitar on *Nothing Would Have Been Any Old Fun At All*. It is the musical genius of Christopher Sessions that runs through these tracks like lettering through Edinburgh rock, and I am deeply grateful to Chris, both for his supreme talent and for his outstanding sense of professionalism in the studio.

Lawson's Sausage
(Hidden track)

The Salome of Hammersmith
Our own Belgravia Belle
Of one thing let's be certain
Nigella's quite the swell!